Love

Rosa Mar

True Love at Last

Rosa Ortiz Marti

WESTBOW
PRESS®
A DIVISION OF THOMAS NELSON
& ZONDERVAN

Copyright © 2016 Rosa Ortiz Marti.

All rights reserved. No part of this book may be used or reproduced by any means, graphic, electronic, or mechanical, including photocopying, recording, taping or by any information storage retrieval system without the written permission of the author except in the case of brief quotations embodied in critical articles and reviews.

Scripture taken from the King James Version of the Bible.

Scripture taken from the *Amplified Bible*, copyright © 1954, 1958, 1962, 1964, 1965, 1987 by The Lockman Foundation. Used by permission.

Scripture taken from the Holy Bible, NEW INTERNATIONAL VERSION®. Copyright © 1973, 1978, 1984, 2011 by Biblica, Inc. All rights reserved worldwide. Used by permission. NEW INTERNATIONAL VERSION® and NIV® are registered trademarks of Biblica, Inc. Use of either trademark for the offering of goods or services requires the prior written consent of Biblica US, Inc.

WestBow Press books may be ordered through booksellers or by contacting:

WestBow Press
A Division of Thomas Nelson & Zondervan
1663 Liberty Drive
Bloomington, IN 47403
www.westbowpress.com
1 (866) 928-1240

Because of the dynamic nature of the Internet, any web addresses or links contained in this book may have changed since publication and may no longer be valid. The views expressed in this work are solely those of the author and do not necessarily reflect the views of the publisher, and the publisher hereby disclaims any responsibility for them.

Any people depicted in stock imagery provided by Thinkstock are models, and such images are being used for illustrative purposes only. Certain stock imagery © Thinkstock.

ISBN: 978-1-5127-3727-1 (sc)
ISBN: 978-1-5127-3728-8 (hc)
ISBN: 978-1-5127-3726-4 (e)

Library of Congress Control Number: 2016905418

Print information available on the last page.

WestBow Press rev. date: 4/28/2016

Contents

Dedication vii
Acknowledgment ix
Introduction xi

Chapter 1: Looking for Love in all the
Wrong Places 1
Chapter 2: Love is not abusive 11
Chapter 3: Love is giving 21
Chapter 4: Learning to love when you don't
feel loved in returned 33
Chapter 5: Discovering The Source of True Love ... 37
Chapter 6: Abide In The Lord 55
Chapter 7: The Necessity of Love 71
Chapter 8: True Love at Last 81

About the Author 95

Dedication

To my wonderful husband Pedro, our children, grandchildren, my parents, and my amazing Sunday School teachers Robin and Glenn Hohman for your love and encouragement all of these years in ministry. Life was indeed a little easier because of the Godly wisdom you all shared with me.

Acknowledgment

I give all the glory and praise to God, for giving me this opportunity to share what He and He alone, has placed in my heart with the world.

Everything I went through was for a reason, the trials, and all the circumstances were so I could grow in the Lord and helped all the people He has placed in my path.

God used Pastor Bill Wilson, Senior pastor of Metro International Church in Brooklyn NY; to introduce me to the true love I was searching for.

And as I decreased in Him daily, I had to learn not to worry about things I'd face through this life's journey. I want to thank my wonderful husband Pedro Marti for loving me in Jesus, for all his encouragement. Also the huge encouragement I received from so many special people in my church FBCWP. My thanks go to: Navy Captain Glenn Hohman, and Robin Baab-Hohman my amazing Bible teachers and encouragers and to Robin for the amazing godly art work she put together for my front cover… Oh' how I love you both so much; to John & Bonnie Mitchell for being my best friends; to Carl & Sylvia Webb, Wanda Irwin Rocky and Judith Carson, David and Margaret Kohs, Gerald and Lyn Richardson, Peggy Wroten, Carl & Rachel Cahill, Coach Friedley, Dr. Eddie and Sandy Waldheim, Ann Anderson, Nancy Moore, and to Hazel, an angel from God! Thanks to all my children and grandchildren; to Jose for always saying, "Mom, you can do it." To Edith, Kristie, Victor, Pedro Jr., Robert, Joshua, Leonel.

Destiny, Elias, Isabela, Joey (Miguelito), Charisma, Nathaniel, Mileena, and Christina, my grandchildren for always telling me that I'm the best grandma in the world!

To Peter Odriscoll (Pastor O) for letting God use you in my life,

Thank you for Loving Jesus! COMPLETE IN JESUS CHRIST!

Introduction

Many times we find ourselves needing something in our lives that will make us complete. Looking for that special someone that will take our breath away. We all want to be happy and complete, but many times we find ourselves alone with no one who is able to fill the void deep in our hearts. Too many people are looking for love in all the wrong places. What is love? Is it that feeling of joy and happiness? Is it the warm feeling inside of you that happens to be indescribable? Or is it the pain that leaves us broken-hearted in the end. Can it be an emotion that gives us hope, but also gives us a detailed picture of our reality? How can one word be the root to so many different emotions? Mankind has given love a title, a title that will never be hard to change in this world. Sometimes man confuses lust for love and hearts are broken. But the Bible tells us that God is love. Presently people are blind to the truth; but the only way to find the true meaning of love, is to know God. Are you ready?

CHAPTER ONE

Looking for Love in all the Wrong Places

A multitude of people is searching for love and acceptance in all the wrong places. Many children have the horrible experience of living life without a father's, or a mother's love, guidance, or teaching. Nevertheless when they reach maturity a void within begins to bother them. After being in ministry for so many years I found out that there is no difference with children who were surrounded by amazing parents all of their lives, because even they too can feel the same void. Every single one of us begins to search for the love we believe we have missed out in life. This is especially true of children of divorce. Many parents are unaware of the damage they cause their children when they decide to divorce or separate. They have the focus on the (me, myself & I syndrome) and forget that there are little children who are counting on them for love, encouragement, and life training. It is clear that our decisions have a ripple effect. Believe me my friend every child needs the love of both parents. Sometimes it can't be helped. Maybe one of them was abandoned by the other, or one passed away, and the other has no choice but to raise their children without a partner. No matter what the situation may have been, a growing child needs the love, direction, godly teaching and care of both parents. If they don't receive these qualities of living, a big void will remain within their hearts.

Let me tell you this story about a unique young girl name Candiz. At the age of two Candiz's life was traumatized when her parents separated. She was heartbroken being away from her daddy; but there was nothing a young child could do at that age. Many nights the pillow became her handkerchief as she cried, not being able to hug her dad goodnight. Eight years after her parents' separation, she tried many different things to get them back together but nothing she did was successful. Candiz's parents separated for good and the horrible day came when they ended their marriage by divorce. She knew this situation created a deep void in her heart. Despite how much she pretended to be unaffected, that emptiness was always there. The word void means Empty, nothing there; having no legal force or effect; useless, ineffectual; vain; no meaning; without contents; vacant; a gap; a vacancy. (Merriam Webster -Dictionary). I just had to use all the definitions of the meaning of void so that you could understand the emptiness experienced by so many people of all ages. We all have a void located deep within our hearts. This void is the main reason people begin to look for love in all the wrong places. What are some ways they search in the wrong places?

Many people have the notion that another person is capable of filling that aching void. Let me tell you that the void within our hearts makes us a target for pain, especially when we don't understand the meaning of it. Eventually, you will end up with a broken heart, when the falling in love business begins. The day will come when you will meet that special person, the one who will walk in "love" with you. Yes, walking in Love is so much better then falling in love. When we walk in love we get to know the person. Initially, these emotions begin to work their way into the heart which causes you to fall in love. The breathing pattern changes; the heart beats faster. At that moment and time, it is a wonderful sensation when you think you have found the person who truly makes you feel complete. Men, women and children all have the same need to be loved, to be hugged, or simply to hear kind, loving words. Nevertheless the bottom line is that on a daily basis people need to know that they are loved.

Many times, when that special person is not spending enough time with us, we'll begin to experience loneliness. The word lonely means: affected with or causing a depressing feeling of being alone; lonesome, destitute of sympathetic or friendly companionship, remote from places of human habitation. Loneliness is a horrible feeling because you will feel lonely even when there are people all around you. One could have a large family and still feel the effects of being lonely. When we are lonely, we lack that personal relationship with someone that shows they care. Many times we all feel lonely even if our homes are full of people. A depressing feeling enters our being, even when we are surrounded by our children, spouse or our friends. The saddest feeling is when we are in a gathering, and you think no one there cares that you are in the room. There are many different reasons why we feel that way; but one thing I do know by experience, we all feel that way because we don't feel loved. Isn't it weird how this happens to so many people around the world? It doesn't matter how many people are around us; there comes a time in our life when we feel lonely. Believe me friend, that is a void that no man, woman, or child can fill!

Many people seem to make so many mistakes looking for true love; but when they think that they have found it, once again it adds up to a big disappointment.

Many times we all get hurt in relationships, but our journey continues. We are determined to find true love. However, after so many mistakes and a broken heart, we realize that this is impossible. Or is it? Everyone is looking for that perfect mate, the one who sweeps you off your feet. At the beginning of any relationship the heart start raising the giggles and the "oh baby, I can't live without you" He/ She takes you in a warm embrace, and you believe that he or she is the one you have been waiting for all of your life. Here comes the wedding day and the promises to love and cherish till death do you part; then the months and the years pass by and the love begins to die out. Wow! What happened to the giggles, the heart pumping, the breathless times you both experienced, and the "Oh Baby I can't live without you?" Oops; it is all gone, so you think. In some relationships too many things happen which cause hurts and heartbreaks between two parties. They forget to apologize to each other and to say those magical words, "I love you". This is where the fear builds that your partner no longer cares for you. You have too many arguments and not enough apologies. Then when you least expect it, here comes that horrible word "Divorce" which God hates so much.

In the Bible, it says that God hates divorce. It was never meant, for two people who made the decision to pledge their love to each other until death, to just wake up one day and decide that it is all over. When you made those vows to each other as a covenant before God, maybe you forgot the last words the minister stated which are, "What God has joined "together" let no man put asunder (Separate)." This promise can never be broken except by death or fornication when you have an unforgiving heart. (Matthews 19:8-9), He saith unto them, "Moses because of the hardness of your hearts suffered you to put away your wives: but from the beginning it was not so. And I say unto you, whosoever shall put away his wife, except it be for fornication, and shall marry another, committed adultery. And whoso married her which is put away doeth commit adultery." It is so important to keep the fire of love burning in your relationship in order to keep it alive. A marriage is not something which happens when you say, "I do." No! A real marriage is one you build day by day. It really takes <u>two</u> to build a strong marriage.

When you and your mate vow and promised to love one another, you are supposed to pick up the tools which are the promises you made to each other, and never forget "Till death do us part." Please remember that, in order for any house to last, it must be built on a strong and firm foundation which is Jesus Christ. "Unless the LORD builds the house, those who build it, labor in vain. Unless the LORD watches over the city, the watchman stays awake in vain." (Psalms 127:1)

The Lord is the glue that keeps that marriage together especially when the Lord is the Lord of both. A very important tool for every relationship is a daily expression of their love for one another in order to keep it alive. A friend of mine told me that when your relationship becomes sour and cold try to remember what was it, about that person which attracted you in the first place; and that will help your relationship. I know sometimes it is hard, dealing with too many people all day long. busyness and taking someone for granted; destroys relationship too.

There are many couples who appeared to have a healthy marriage; but the appearance is sadly far from the truth. Couples who are married dedicated to working hard outside of their home. Sometimes lack the understanding of relational communication with their spouse. Several factors are to blame. People will use exhaustion; or that they have dealt with too many people, and it has been a long day of work as an excuse not to communicate. When this situation continues for a number of years. It will put a strain on their marriage.

Many wives are the kind of women who wait for the husband to make the first move, and never say anything to him about the situation which is pulling them apart. What is one of the biggest mistakes many married women commit? Women have the tendency to think that their spouse knows what they are thinking, or what they are feeling inside. Believe me communication is very important! How can they know unless we tell them?

Being distant for a long period of time, destroys relationships. As human beings, we need closeness. Communication is the key; but most importantly, understanding of what the other party is going through is a true blessing for every marriage. Sometimes busyness doesn't let us see the good qualities of the person we say we love. Spouses only see the good qualities of a partner when they take time to observe the good things they do, instead of concentrating on all their faults. It is so sad that some marriages start realizing what they have only when they are forced to sit a little longer because of their old age, or because some illness has hit their lives.

Don't ever ignore the person who chose to share their life with you. Sometimes a person doesn't express love in words but they do in deeds; therefore remember that most people need to hear "I love you" all the time. Don't ever take anyone for granted! Show your love and take time daily to say those wonderful words: "I Do Love You"! We will be surprised what those simple words can do to that special person we are sharing our life with. Don't make the same mistake many people do, in keeping all the love inside. Remember that no one else can read your thoughts. Do your best to take good care of what God has given you. If the person is giving you everything which is needed to live a good life do the same for them. That is what sharing a life all is about!

CHAPTER TWO

Love is not abusive

> What does it take for us to realize the value within us? We are all fearfully and wonderfully made. "I praise you because I am fearfully and wonderfully made; your works are wonderful, I know that full well." (Psalm 139:14 NIV)

Oh, how hard it is to hear that someone is being abused by a spouse, parent or just by anyone, in particular. The worst mistake is when the abused chooses to continue to live in an abusive relationship. When I think about all the horrible stories I've have heard in my life, being in ministry for twenty-seven years, makes me very upset. It's horrible to experience living with an abusive person for many years. Just thinking that they love you; but love is never abusive. Sometimes people argue for the dumbest things and physical abuse begins. What to do when this occurs? Many of us have a forgiving heart, when they come asking to be forgiven, we just do. Many times we feel like there is no way out. Because of this, we continue to go on with our normal routine every week, and no one will have any idea of what we are experiencing in our lives. This situation is truly abuse, mistaken for love.

No person has the right to cause you bodily injury, especially someone who swears they love you. God never wants us to remain in a situation of violence. Speak to someone; get help; don't be silent! It takes a lot to make the first move to go and get help; but for the sake of the children and for our own safety, we must take the courage to run. Sometimes we think a lot about our children and we don't want to separate them from the family unit, but if you are being physically abused, please get help. And for those who are being sexually abused and who feel threatened, find someone that you can trust and speak to them. We are wonderfully made, don't ever forget that. All of the abuse which many individuals endured when they were young creates in them a passion to protect their own children. Be attentive as you read this story about Candiz.

Candiz grew up to be a lovely young woman who was struggling with many challenges. Despite a troubled marriage, she was the mother of four children and pregnant with her fifth. Irreconcilable difference had required her to separate from their father, so she was now a single mother who adored her children. Nevertheless, she was so happy because her children were everything to her. Her love for the children was too intense! She loved them more than anything, even more than she loved God. When she least expected it, something horrible happened. Her children were taken away from her for a time, but for Candiz it was an eternity. Not to be able to be with them was devastating. During that time everyone forsook her, and she found herself on her knees crying unto God. She felt so alone because everyone had turn their backs on her. She was finally forced to focus on the true God of heaven. Candiz became aware of God's presence like never before. She understood what it meant to love God with all of her hearts, soul and mind. She had to be apart from her children whom she loved more than anything, to discover that God is Who He said He is. How did all this happen?

It came about on a day when there was a knock on the door. It was Candiz's sister, whom she hadn't seen for over ten years. Candiz was so excited to see her again! They talked for a while before the sister asked Candiz to go out with her. Candiz needed a babysitter. She asked a neighbor if she would babysit the children. The neighbor agreed. Candiz was so excited when they left the house for a special time just between two sisters.

After a few hours of enjoying her sister's company Candiz received a call. She was shocked. Something was wrong with her children. Someone had removed her children from their home. Candiz felt a horrible pain in her heart, as she rushed to find her children. She felt hopeless; she had to wait all weekend to speak with the agency which had taken her children. It was the longest weekend of her life. She spent the whole weekend on her knees imploring God to help her. Finally, Monday came. She went to the Agency's building, where, after an hour of waiting, a caseworker assigned to her called her into the office.

The lady was very kind. She said that in all her years of working with the department, she have never seen such well-behaved children. She explained to Candiz that they had taken all the children to the hospital, and all the reports had come out good. There were no signs of abuse. Also Caseworker was surprised to learn that none of the children knew the meaning of being punished. The social worker explained to her that Candiz was going to court where it was up to the Judge as to what would happen to the children. Candiz began to cry and felt so hopeless. It was not fair that she had to wait for a court date; meanwhile who knows where or with whom her kids were staying? The caseworker said that the two boys were with a foster family in one home, and the two girls were with another family. Candiz pleaded with her to place them together in a safe, loving home. Little did she know that her eldest son was also asking the foster parent the same thing? The social worker stated that she would do everything in her power to put the four children in the same house until the investigation was complete. She promised Candiz, that she would work as fast as she could and that hopefully Candiz would be able to get her children's back at the end of that week.

The frustration was overwhelming. She cried and spent a lot of time on her knees praying to God. Throughout many horrible instances that occurred through that time of not being with her children, she came to understand who God was and is. She was broken through the grace of God.

Candiz's sister came over to say she was sorry for everything Candiz was going through, but when her sister left, and Candiz was again left all alone to deal with her situation. She began to pray. "Jesus help me; God please, you are the only One that can help me!" For days she continue praying to God. Thoughts of loving her children, more than anything or anyone, kept coming into her mind. God took away from her the one thing that she'd loved more than Him. But something amazing happened to Candiz, there on her knees she asked God to forgive her. At that moment, she understood the power of God and His authority over her life. He was number one, and no one else was going to be more important than Him. He showed her that nobody, not even her family was going to move a finger to help her unless she enter the realization of whom He was.

Candiz remembered hurting so much, kneeling by her bed all alone, crying and begging the Lord to give her back her children. After several days on her knees' she understood what "loving God with all of her heart" meant; therefore she got up from the floor and got ready for church. While in church she stood up to worship and praise the Lord. The pastor was amazed that in her circumstances she still was able to worship, not bitter, or angry at God. At that moment, her understanding was that no one, but God was able to give her back her children (Matthew 22:37). After church, it was time to go back home by herself. Walking into that empty apartment the silence overwhelmed her and again she knelt beside her bed, crying and praying all night long.

The next day she went to see her children. It was just an hour visit, and it went by so fast! She told her eldest son to take care of his little brother and his two sisters and not to worry; because God would return them back home very soon. Candiz felt so much energy;

she decided to decorate the children's room with toys before they got home. It was like all her worries and concerns had disappeared. She stopped by a toy store and bought all kinds of toys for the children. As she was going toward the cash register, her eye spotted a funny monkey on a rope. She said to herself, "I know my big boy will love this monkey". Candiz ran home, she'd began to decorate her children's room with all the toys and the monkey. With so much love she arranged it all until everything looked very beautiful and ready for the arrival of her children. Finally the day came when Candiz was to be reunited with her precious children.

Every time there was a knock at the door she ran toward it. First it was her sister, then other people and suddenly she began to worry when she looked at the clock she'd noticed it was twelve midnight. Her tears began to roll down her face, but she will never forget that exactly at 12:30 am, there was a knock on the door. As soon as she opened the door all four of her children ran in, laughing and hugging. Candiz children were finally home! They spent all night talking about everything they had experienced at the foster home, but at last they were all home.

Candiz couldn't believe everything that they had to endure; but one thing she was sure of was that she would never leave them with anyone ever again. This time Candiz now understood that she'd loved God first, more than anyone or anything. Many children are taken from their parents because they are abused or neglected; nevertheless Candiz children were returned to her in two and a half weeks. All the evidence showed that they came from a loving family and they were never abused. However it was when Candiz surrendered completely to God, everything worked out. Children are a blessing from the Lord; abusing them is a horrible thing. Abuse is never Love.

Many woman and men today are living in an abusive relationship, and they don't know how to get out. Everyone has a desire to be loved, but when we get abused by the person that is supposed to love and protect us, a hurt grows within us which nobody else can ever understand. Many times loving compassion blurs our thinking. When that person who caused the abuse comes back and asks you to forgive them, you just do! This is wrong. The truth is, when we are in love, many times it affects the way we think. Take this from me if you are being abused, you don't have to take it any longer. Yes, we need to be loved but not that way. An abusive person is a sick person, and whoever it might be, he or she is in a great need of help!

If it were not for God's word, many of us would have never learned to be free. Sometimes, fear overtakes us, just thinking of what could happen to us if we leave the person who has cause us so much harm. What would that person do to us if we do leave? If you want the abuse to stop, you must make your move "now". There are so many places where you can go and get help if you are being abused by your partner. Every time he or she returns with a mouth full of apologies and the announcement that he or she loves you... Do Not Be Fooled! If a person truly loves another person a partner will never cause harm. The word abuse means "to use wrongly, improperly, or cruelty on people or animal. To say hurtful or rude things to or about someone; to put to wrong use: to abuse one's privileges."

When I noticed so many people going through abusive situations, and people looking for love in all the wrong places, I finally decided to start this book and help as many people as I can. I want to help you from suffering the abuse that many of us suffered for so many years. Remember that we are all fearfully and wonderfully made by an amazing God in Heaven!

CHAPTER THREE

Love is giving

For God so loved the world, that he gave his only begotten son, that whosoever believes in him will not perish but have eternal life (John 3:16) KJV.

Wow, what a love Father God has for us, to give his only son to die for somebody else! Can you imagine giving up your only child? I cannot fathom the love God has for us. What is the meaning of this love we all need to know? The amazing love of God for sinful mankind, a love that no one deserves. What is "love" you might ask? Not that we love God, but that he loved us and sent his son as an atoning sacrifice for our sins. (1John 4:10) God is love. (1John 4:8) Love does no harm to its neighbor. Therefore, love is the fulfillment of the law. (Romans 13:10). According to the dictionary, love, is described as, "A strong feeling of affection, and concern for a person such as a mother's love for her children. An emotional, romantic feeling toward a member of the opposite sex. A strong, feeling of friendship for a member of the same sex." Greater love has no one than this; that one lay down his life for his friends (John 15:13).

Love is an <u>action</u> word. What do I mean when I say an action word? Not everyone who states, I love you truly, means it. Sometimes you are placed in a compromising situation when the person you love wants you to prove your love in a sexual way. That is not the action necessary to prove to someone that you love them. However, it is not enough to say you love someone; you need to show it in ways which will <u>not</u> compromise you and your morals.

Many times days go by without you hearing those beautiful words, "I love you"; or without receiving an act of love. If this continues, you'll begin to feel lonely and loveless. Then you will begin to assume that you are not being loved by the one you have chosen. You are not sharing lives. The love action begins to stop. Showing our love, and the relationship begins to fall apart. The sad thing about this situation is that both are at fault. Both have allowed the sparks which began the relationship to vanish.

When we fall in love with someone, there is something which gives us the energy to do for them the impossible if we were able to accomplish it. However, as days, months years have come and gone; the fire that we first felt is gone. The problem with this situation is that people don't know what they have until their partner leaves. Nevertheless when an individual realizes they have taken the chosen person, for granted, and suddenly that person walks out, they are devastated. We must understand this: <u>Love is an action word.</u> If you feel it go ahead, express it. Action speaks louder than words. Action is the process of doing things. We must do things from the heart for the ones we say we love. Women have a need to be loved and to be understood. It is amazing, but true.

In the book of Ephesians 5:25 it says, "Husband loves your wives, even as Christ also loved the church, and gave himself for it." When the husband loves his wife and shows his love to her, the woman concentrates on being a better helper to him. Nevertheless, she will make sure that all of his needs at home are met. With men, it is different; because the way women need to show their husband love is by respecting him. There is a special scripture in the Bible which says, "Nevertheless, let every one of you in particular so love his wife even as himself. And the wife sees that she reverence (deep respect) her husband" (Ephesians 5:33 KJV). When a man is not being respected, he can't function the way God intends for him to function. The reason I say this is because some women are always talking down to their husbands. This kind of situation destroys relationships.

Many people do not know any of these principles. However, if they did know them, I don't think it would make a difference if they are victims of abuse. All I know is that when the person you love is physically abusive… you must get away as soon as you can; because God does not want us to live in danger. (Love is kind 1 Corinthian 13:4) When an abusive spouse decides to leave, you must let the unbelieving spouse depart. We know that it takes strong courage and determination on our part to be free from that bondage of abuse; nevertheless it is not easy. But after much prayer, and by putting our trust in God to help us through it all, every single day it will become easier.

It takes much faith to keep walking forward and never look back. Some do this by keeping busy and not giving themselves time to think about the missing partner. Some have to flood themselves with work, and with Bible Studies to renew their minds. I will fail to tell you the truth if I say that taking a stand for yourself and your children is not hard! All I know today is that, God will be there for us, every step of the way. When we finally make that decision to flee from constant mistreatment it will be at that moment that we let go, and let God take over our heart and emotions.

God is right there with us; He will never leave us, nor forsake us, just like the Bible it says in Deuteronomy 31:6, "Be strong and courageous. Do not be afraid or terrified because of them, for the Lord your God goes with you; he will never leave you nor forsake you."

Every day will become better and easier. Candiz experienced this when she began to pray a special petition to God, asking Him to remove the void she felt in her heart. God gave her a strong desire to study the Bible, and she began growing in love with God more than anything in this world. She felt that God gave her another opportunity to have the right relationship with Him. He gave her back the children and delivered her from difficult situations in her life. God gave her peace in her heart about everything. God also provided for every physical need she had. After all those years Candiz found herself being a single mother with five children and it was okay, because God was very near to her. She knew He was there for her and her children every step of the way. Her heart was finally being healed. There are many Candizes out there. We thank you, Lord for never leaving Candiz alone, in that storm of life. She now had time to devote herself to her children and to getting a Christian education. She began to volunteer at church, reaching out to the needy and broken in communities of New York City. But she still felt that something was missing.

One morning during her prayer time she asked God for true love? When she finished praying, she got up off her knees and went to work, but she felt so depressed. Candiz arrived at work, looking for something to do. She asked her department leader to give her a lot of work so she could distract herself. That particular day she felt like cleaning, so she'd asked for the dirtiest place in the property. So she could spend a long time by herself. The leader of her department smiled and said, "Okay Candiz, Go cleaned the sound room". Not thinking much about anything, she'd proceeded to the sound room. She was so amazed to see how dirty that place was!

She began to clean, but after filling three large bags with garbage, Candiz didn't have any idea how she was going to remove it by herself. She looked down the steep ladder that took her up to the sound room. Thinking to herself, "How in the world am I going to get down from here?" the answer came. The Bible says that; every good gift and every perfect gift is from above, and cometh down from the Father (James 1:17) KJV. (Soon you will know what I meant by this verse)

After a short while of trying to figure out how she was going to get down, the back door of the place opened. She was ecstatic when one of the Sunday school department leader, walked in. Immediately she asked him if he would be so kind as to help her with three bags full of garbage. Being a gentleman, he came up the steep ladder and carried down all the huge bags full of garbage. Although Candiz and the gentleman had seen each other at the church for three years, they had never talked to one another before.

They were attending the same church both got saved in the same month and year. They also were baptized on the same day, but they had never said a word to one another until this day. (Sometimes we need to be careful what we ask God for; because He sometimes has a sense of humor in the way he answer's our prayers.) Candiz was looking for true love, and God send her a man who was living a loveless and troubled life. That day was the beginning of a wonderful friendship. He was very friendly to Candiz, and treated her with much respect. He was a little too good to be true, but Candiz enjoyed his attentions. So they got to know each other better. They talked for hours in the phone every single day, just talking about simple things that mattered in their lives. They prayed together every single day, and also shared Bible Studies over the telephone each evening.

Candiz was so impressed of how much her new friend knew about the scriptures. The two of them would spend hours talking about the Bible. Little by little they got to know, and build a relationship with each other. What a difference in comparison to her previous relationship. After a while, he asked her for a date, but she was hesitant because their relationship was always over the phone, and she was afraid of even thinking about being with anyone. After a while, he kept insisting, so she agreed. He picked up Candiz in a beautiful red sports car and took her to a romantic place for dinner. He was such a gentleman they had such a wonderful time together. He was so different from the father of her children. With much respect, he wanted to get to know her, and the children. He didn't care that Candiz had five children. They would always go on outings as a family. Most of the times he invited them to the beach, and they all went. One day he noticed that she would just wet her feet, and he tried to pull her into the water. Candiz was terrified of the beach, because many years before she had a near drowning experience. He gently held her by the hands and told her to trust him that he would not let her go. She hesitated just a little, but looking into his eyes he said again, "Trust me." And she did! After that day her fears of the ocean disappeared; Candiz began to swim again. The gentlemen was raising a child on his own, and together with her five children they always had a lot of fun.

They continued to be friends. Every day after work he would call her, but sometimes she had to do something for her children. This meant they had to stop talking for a while; but to her surprise the next day he gave her a gift? Oh my, when she opened it you will not believe what was in the package? A 200 foot Telephone cord. He said, "Now when you have to do something you don't have to get off the phone." "Um okay". One day after work, he asked her if she wanted to go meet his mother & sister. He said that his sister and mother wanted to meet her, but at first she hesitated, then he kept insisting, so Candiz when ahead and agreed to go. His sister and mother welcomed her so warmly.

His sister brought out a jewelry catalog, and her gentleman asked her to choose a diamond ring!

She felt awkward but began to go through the pages, which indeed had so many beautiful, very expensive diamond rings. In her heart, she felt so nervous, that in her mind she wanted to run out of that house. But she didn't want to embarrass him in front of his family. She pointed to the most expensive ring in the catalog, because she honestly thought that there was no way he could afford it. Then after a delightful time with his mother and sister he took her home. That night he called her and told her, that "God told me that you are going to be my wife!"

Candiz rapidly responded, "How did God tell you such a thing?" He read a passage from the Bible and explained that God had indeed spoked, to him. She was dumbfounded, but they ended the conversation with a prayer and said good night!

The following day, Candiz had planned a trip to a theme park with her Royal Ranger's class, which is a boy's group similar to Boy Scouts. She needed a driver, and her gentleman agreed to drive the bus for her. When they got to the Great Adventure Park, they began to walk and enjoy the beautiful park. There in the middle of this park, He began to tell her how much he loved her. Right there in the middle of the Adventure Park he proposed to her. To her surprise, he put the ring she had chosen from the catalog on her finger, "She was in shock."

Fear came over Candiz; she didn't want to enter into another marital relationship. But that day they had such a wonderful time it really became a great adventure. He brought his son with them and on that day, this child began to call her mom. After a long day they headed home. Soon after getting home. Candiz stared at the beautiful ring he had just put on her finger; but she began to tremble and decided to take it off her finger.

The following day she went to all her classes in Bible College and then as she was entering the work office she saw him. He approached her quickly. He was so sweet that she felt his pain, as she returned the ring and said that she was sorry. She explained she was not ready to enter into a marriage relationship. He made a promised to her that everything was going to be different, to give him a try.

She felt bad, but told him not to rush into anything at that point. She stated "let's just continue to get to know each other better." So he agreed. Day after day they would go out together with their children. To their surprise, all of their children got along great. But Candiz was terrified to start something new. He again told her that God had revealed to him, that she was going to be his wife.

Again he proposed and put the ring on her finger, but again she said "No." He proposed on two more occasions. On the fourth proposal, before she answered, he stated, "This time, this is the <u>last</u> time I am going to asked you." She began to smile. At that moment gazing, into the eyes of her sweet gentlemen, she thought to herself, "Wow is this the true love, the kind I have been looking for all of my life?"

December 28, 1991 Candiz, and her darling husband joined together in the sight of God. Together they were learning that Love is giving- not only to each other, but also to everyone they encounter in their walk with Jesus.

CHAPTER FOUR

Learning to love when you don't feel loved in returned

I love you, O LORD, my strength. (Psalm 18:1)

Candiz began her new life together with her husband. She lived every single day for the first year of marriage, enjoying all the attention her husband gave her. Every day he took the time to call her, to say how much he loved her. Which it was one of his promises that he made to Candiz when he first proposed to her. Candiz and her husband started working together doing ministry, helping the homeless get off the street. They would rescue homeless men and women and place them in two different residential properties that they had purchased. At that time, they were not able to spend much time together, because of their busy schedules. Candiz was suffering from a horrible feeling of loneliness. She reminded him of all the promises he made to her when they got engaged. He couldn't understand why she would feel lonely when she was surrounded by so many people.

He was focusing on the homeless ministry more than his family. Here, even though she was married to a Christian man she was feeling lonely and loveless again. Candiz had imagined her life being different; however, although she was not physically abused, but she was feeling very unloved. She resented the fact that something else's had taken her husband's attention away. Candiz didn't know how to handle that situation, and her emotions ran wild, especially when she wanted to do what was right for her husband. Every day she reminisced on the first year of their marriage and how wonderful it was, just like a fairy-tale story. Candiz started to concentrate on the things that she loved about her husband. For example the times when he taught her how to study the Bible, their intimate prayer time, and the new family time teaching their children about the Bible every week.

Deep down Candiz was missing the children ministry she had been involved in. before she got married. It broke her heart when she had to leave that place. Her place of refuge, the place where she was led to Jesus as her savior. She received teaching; that helped her to persevere when she went through hard times. Nobody was aware of Candiz secret pain; as she began to work with her husband at the Homeless ministry. She was so miserable and angry no one knew the pain she had in her heart. She tried to make the best of the situation; but with no one knowing every week she would call her former church to find out how things were going. She just wanted to stay connected in some way.

Candiz and her husband spend less and less time together. He always said he was too busy doing something, and she tried to understand because he was helping the homeless after all. Day by day, he woke up very early to get to the ministry. He was the Assistant Director, and he was in charge of the program. For a moment Candiz understood that he did, indeed, have a lot of responsibilities. Candiz needed to understand how to control all of her emotions. She buried herself studying the Bible; she learned to love her husband even when things didn't go well. In the Bible it says, "And when we have known and believed the love God has to us, God is love, and he that dwelleth in love dwelleth in God and God in him." 1 John- 4:16 (KJV).

Candiz had to learn to trust God, even when the circumstances were not easy.

In the first few years of their marriage, Many times they argued for foolish reasons; then she would make him laugh so he could smile again. Looking back to her past, Candiz believes that even when she tried to start a new life with her husband, deep down, she felt messed-up about everything. Her prior life situation had left scars... The saddest part for Candiz was discovering that now she didn't know how to handle any disagreement between the two of them. An abusive relationship destroys people from within, especially when you remain in the abusive situation for years.

Anger and hurt builds inside of those who once were abused, even when they believe they are free. Our memory of everything that has occurred will continue to come back; therefore it took Candiz a very long time for her to recover from that horrible ordeal. Years later she could say "I am a survivor" and became a defender, encourager of women that were going through the same thing. For all the young men and women out there, please take your time in getting into a serious relationship, don't ever rush into anything. Make sure that you get to know well, the person you are dating before you get engaged; seek God for wisdom and directions and make sure you do hear from God before you make a commitment, because your decision will have an effect on the rest of your life.

CHAPTER FIVE

Discovering The Source of True Love

Beloved, if God so loved us, we ought also
to love one another. (1 John 4:11, KJV).

For the first few years of marriage, Candiz became very accustomed to the attention her husband gave her. But when he started working in the homeless shelter he became too busy, so they began to have many arguments. Candiz began to experience a horrible feeling of loneliness and anger. One day as she was praying on her knees, she began to cry unto the Lord saying that she wanted to be happy, and truly loved. She was on her knees for a long period of time, when all of a sudden the Lord answered her. "Man will never give you the love that you need, want, or sought for all these years." He said, "I have loved you with an everlasting love, Love that has no end. A love that never changes" He continued by saying to Candiz, that some people love for a time. Man's love changes almost all the time, but the love that comes from Him never changes.

On that day Candiz cried like a baby. On her knees suddenly she experienced deep within her heart, a love that she had never felt before. It was so amazing! God's love and presence surrounded her and on that moment she understood that for the prior three years of serving Him, she didn't even know Him at all. But now she experienced a touch from Him.

The Lord let her know that never again would she feel lonely or loveless, as long as she abides in His presence daily. Ever since that personal encounter with the Lord, Candiz just changed her whole perspective on life. She continued to live her life by never expecting something from her husband, anyone or anything, which now she knew only God could give her. John 3:16 says, "For God so loved the world that He gave His only begotten son for whosoever believe in Him shall not perish but will inherit everlasting life." KJV. He loves us so much that He gave His son to die on the cross for you and me. That is love that someone would lay down his life in order for us to live. Wow!

Candiz's life with her husband was rough. Their lives became a journey of two people where the only thing they had in common was the love they both shared for the Lord Jesus Christ. Candiz truly believes that only the love they both shared for the Lord Jesus Christ was the glue that kept them together after all those years. She also learned that a man is capable of loving in a very deep way when he has Jesus as his Lord and Savior in his heart.

Her search for love was over. She knew that her husband could never love her the way she wanted, because that love only came from God. Many years have passed, Candiz and her husband moved to the suburbs. They struggled a little trying to figure each other out. They were so different, and that made it difficult for them to get along. One thing was for sure, Candiz and her husband had a strong desire to serve God. They both agreed to open a Marketing business. From the proceeds of the business, they were able to buy their home. After that, they purchased two big houses, one for homeless men, and the other for homeless women and children.

By this time Candiz became so busy that she didn't schedule for what was important any longer, like spending quality time with God; but she had to learn the hard way. Three years went by. She was so busy trying to serve God in the children's and homeless ministries that she couldn't even take one second to speak to God. Beloved, when God wants you to do something believe me when I tell you. He will get your attention someway or somehow. There is a story in the Bible about this man named Jonah. God send him to Nineveh, to preach to the Ninevites because their wickedness had come before the Lord. "But Jonah rose one morning and fled to Tar-shish from the presence of the Lord. And went down to Joppa; He found a ship going to Tar-shish, so he paid the fare because of that. And went down into it to go with them, unto Tar-shish from the presence of the Lord. But the Lord sends a great wind into the sea, and there was a mighty tempest in the sea so that the ship was about to be broken. Then the mariners were afraid, and cried every man unto his God, and cast forth the wares that were in the ship into the sea, to lighten it of them. Jonah was gone down into the sides of the ship; he lay and was fast asleep. So the shipmaster came to him, what meanest thou, Oh Sleeper? Arise, call upon thy God, and if so be that God will think upon us, that we perish not. And they said everyone to his fellow, come and let us cast lots, and the lots fell upon Jonah." (Jonah 1 KJV)

Jonah disobeyed God. Everyone on the ship was in danger of perishing. To make this story short, they pushed Jonah overboard, and then a big fish swallowed him, he remained three days in the belly of the whale. Jonah got on his knees and prayed. There he asked God to forgive him and to give him another chance. God heard his prayers then caused the whale to vomit him up on the beach. Jonah then went on to Nineveh and did what the Lord had commanded him to do. The reason I write about this story is because something similar happened to Candiz. The first time she'd heard from the Lord, to write this book she found herself always too busy, so she didn't have time to write anything. Things began to happen to her. Candiz will never forget that one night when she had to pick up her oldest son from work. Prior to leaving her house she received a call from her mother asking Candiz to relay a message to her brother. She agreed to relate the message. Her husband for some reason became agitated and said to Candiz not to go, but she got offended and argued with him. Now when she looks back at that night, Candiz says she should of have listened to her husband!

She knows because when she finished delivering the message to her brother something horrible happened. As Candiz and her son was driving away she looked in her rearview mirror, and saw a red car just speeding behind them. Suddenly her van was picked up from the impact of the car crashing against the back window. The force of the hit made the two front seats rip off the van. Candiz remembered the shout that came out of her son's mouth with horror, "Mom, stop the van!" The perpetrator sped away, and until this day he has never been found.

Candiz's son was very lucky, because he didn't get hurt, but she was not that fortunate. After that accident she had to have surgery to repair her right shoulder. Two weeks after the surgery, she began to feel so sick with fevers of 104 degrees. Never in her life did Candiz ever felt so much pain all over her body. The horrible feeling of being sick for a long period of time was immensely disrupting her thinking. She decided to call her father, he rushed to her side, and took Candiz to the hospital. Her pain was so intense, but the symptoms were misdiagnosed mistakenly for the flu. She was discharged, and send home. The horrible pain got worse day and night at this point it was unbearable .Candiz's husband took her to the hospital again. He was very concerned about her. As soon as they got there, she was rushed back to the emergency room.

Again the doctors misdiagnosed her and she was sent home. When you go through something like this, you can't understand the reason of why God has permitted this to happen to you. Candiz was in so much pain that every step she took felt like her bones were breaking. The next day her husband took her to a different hospital, and again they said it was the Flu without doing a proper diagnosis.

This situation made her very angry. Deep down inside she was praying to God for help. She desperately wanted to get rid of the pain. As she entered her home and began to walk up to her room every step she took felt horrible, with excruciating pain all over her body. Candiz cried out in pain and the following day as she'd remember, it still brings chills to her spine. Because on that fourth day of having high fevers and horrible pain, another frightening thing happened. Now Candiz was not able to even get up from the bed by herself. It brought back memories' of a time years earlier when she thought she was in control of her life. God gave her an assignment, and she didn't listen. Candiz was too busy serving Him and no time to listen to His instructions, so she fail to complete the special assignment He had given her. For many years, she was always doing things for others. Helping people in ministry, teaching, and preaching, the word of God. Now she found herself confined to her bed, not understanding what was happening. But she thanked God that her wonderful husband was there by her side. Candiz, became desperate trying to figure out what was wrong. She remembered saying over and over, "my God, what is wrong with me?" She remembered weeks before when she was teaching their congregation about faith, teaching them about staying strong no matter what situation came their way. Now, there Candiz sat not able to understand at that moment what was going on with her. She thought that by helping many and teaching the word of God, she would always be ok. (But in that moment she knew that bad things happen to everyone under the sun, no one is exempt.

She had made a big mistake that Christians all over the world make. We get too busy serving God, that when he tries to get our attention we are too busy to hear His directions of what He wants us to accomplish for him. On that fourth day of pain and high fevers, and even knowing that she was not able to do things for herself, she became so angry. She was laying on her bed not able to do anything but hurt all over. Candiz began experiencing all these different feelings, and so many thoughts going through her mind. She asked her husband to help her get up. She remembered that as he was helping her stand up, she began to scream out in pain. Her husband wanted to help her, but at that time she wanted to go and do something by herself. (Some of us call that pride)

She began to walk very slowly screaming out in pain, her husband lovingly held her all the way to the bathroom. Her husband saw the agony that she was in and tried to help her, but she rejected his help. Candiz was not able to accept whatever was happening to her. And as she entered the bathroom crying and screaming in excruciating pain. She asked God what she had done. To deserve what was happening to her. Crying for who knows how long, Candiz was in agony she will never forget. Again and again she kept asking God to tell her what she did? "Lord, I'm your servant. What have I done wrong"? The reason she asked God that question was because she truly believed that sick people were not able to minister to anybody. So she believed that her life in ministering to others was over. She had the misconception; that sick people can never pray for others that were also sick. So at that moment she felt broken and confused. It was so hard to remember how long Candiz was in that bathroom. But all we know is that she finally heard God telling her, that her sickness was not unto death. "But that it was for His glory" God permitted the devil to touch her body with this sickness, but not to kill her. She remembered crying uncontrollably. Her husband came in and took her back to their bedroom and gently helped her get into bed. Candiz, cried herself to sleep, but the worst part is that the following day she found herself paralyzed from pain which had made her body stiff. The phone rang. It was her mother announcing that she was on her way to the house. She told Candiz's husband that she was going to find a good hospital which could take good care of her daughter.

Her husband had already called an ambulance. Candiz was concerned about the paramedics carrying her down the stairs. Her husband said not to worry about it, but she began to cry again. Her father and stepmother heard her crying and came into her bedroom. Her dad understood what she was experiencing at that moment. He said to Candiz husband let us all help her go down the stairs. Candiz husband and stepmother finished getting her dressed, and then they all began to pull her up off the bed. Every movement she made going down those stairs felt like she was about to die. Her father put a sheet around her waist to hold her up. One in each side, and her father holding up the sheet. Little by little, step by step, all the way down crying in pain. She looked at them and realized that they too were all crying. It was taking forever for them to get down the stairs. When finally they made it to the first floor, her father put a chair next to the door so she could sit down and wait for the ambulance. As they slowly helped her to the chair, she screamed in horrible, excruciating pain. It was like every bone in her body was broken.

When the ambulance finally arrived, Candiz's mom walked into the house with tears rolling down her cheeks. The paramedics came in, and quickly began to check her blood pressure and determined she didn't have one. They went on to check her pulse and were amazed to find out she didn't have a pulse either. They looked at each other and began to say how can this woman be talking? They rushed her to the hospital. As soon as they took her into the emergency room, the attending physician examined her and ordered all kinds of test. The attending physician was puzzled because according to her it was the first time she took care of a patient that was conscious without a pulse. Every time they tried checking her blood pressure they couldn't get a reading, they began to name her "The Mystery Case". Many curious doctors surrounded Candiz trying to figure out what was wrong with her. When the blood results came back, it showed that she had what was called an "operating room infection" called Sepsis.

After so many tests they rushed her up to the heart monitoring floor, as they discover that she had a heart murmur too. They continued to order blood cultures and many other tests. Many days went by, and they were very concerned because they still were not able to determine what was wrong with her. After a few more days, they transferred Candiz to the Cancer Unit. She began to ask them why they had transferred her to that floor. Was it because they discovered that she had Cancer? Her doctor told her that they were waiting for more results, and that they still didn't know what was wrong with her. After two weeks and four days, they called a new doctor to come see her. This doctor came into her hospital room. He had beautiful ocean blue eyes. As he was examining her he asked her a series of questions, then ordered the nurse to give her some special medication. After an hour she began to move again, the pain was fifty percent gone. Candiz was ecstatic, and she began to praise the Lord as she began to move her legs, her arms, and fingers. She called her husband and began to shout with joy. She told him "honey I can move my body." Her husband was so happy for her, and began to praise the Lord. But after three weeks two doctors entered her hospital room. Candiz was nervous when the doctors began to speak; they stated we have good news and bad news for you, which one do you want first? She said give me the good news first. They said "you don't have Cancer." She said that was great. Then she asked so what is the bad news? He said you had Lupus! "Candiz asked them, what in the world is Lupus? He explained to her that Lupus is a disease that turns your protective system against you, and when it is active, it is very dangerous because it could kill you.

She was devastated! She immediately called her husband and gave him the bad news. He never heard anything about Lupus. He said that he would do research to find out more about Lupus.

After a while, he called her back crying. He told her that he found out everything about the disease, but he changed the conversation, by saying that some family members were coming to see her. Candiz felt fear for the first time in her Christian walk with God. She began to cry uncontrollably. So many things came to her mind. Several hours later her parents and friends arrived. She was amazed that the hospital let every one of them come in to see her. The hospital room was full of people with sad faces. In that moment she had a choice to cry and boohoo all over the place, or be strong. Candiz, was the kind of person that always encouraged people, so she had to be strong for them.

There she was in the hospital bed, overwhelmed with different emotions. One of her family members said, "Just know we love you so much," and gave her a little bear that was praying on his knees. That made her so happy. She looked at them and told them not to worry about her because God was not finished with her yet. She stated that there was still so much that she had to do for God. After a long visit everyone left, and there she stood just meditating on the Lord. The phone rang it was her Pastor, the man that lead her to Christ. He said, "Hey kiddo how are you doing?" Her heart was filled with much joy because he is always traveling and preaching in different countries, and he took the time from his busy schedule to give her a call. He encouraged her with strong words and said to keep on staying strong in the Lord no matter what happens. Candiz felt her spirit renewed as she began again to write her book. The time of going home to her family became a glorious day of praise and worship. She was so grateful to God, because she felt that he gave her another opportunity to walk and move again by herself. When she got home, everything was different the joy of being able to move her legs, her arms, and going up the stairs to her bedroom was a miracle. As the days went passed by, little by little again she became very busy and once again the writing of her book was delayed.

Every time Candiz, neglected spending more time with the Lord or the writing of her book, something went wrong. She began to get sick again and for three years found herself in and out of the hospital. Every time she ended up in the hospital she wrote many amazing life-transforming Bible studies. But every time she got better and was sent home she stop writing her book. Candiz husband convinced her to close the business and to concentrate more on the ministry. She gave up a very successful business and devoted her entire life on just reaching the lost with the gospel of Jesus Christ. In the beginning she continued to get sick.

After so many health complications, she was lucky to be alive. Her Doctor said that she was too young to be going through all that was happening to her. She remembers being on so many medications, that even after everything she was going through; she became addicted to pain medication. Candiz just did not care about anything anymore. Depression set in; nevertheless all their worldly possessions were not important to her. Candiz, felt that she had lost everything, because she listened to her husband and nothing was important to her anymore. The little energy she had left was used to continue the Children ministry.

One day Candiz's doctor informed her that she had to leave New York and go to a warmer climate like Florida or Puerto Rico. That meant that she had to leave the ministry. Candiz felt that everything was over for her. Just the thought of leaving them was like dying completely. The horrible disease "Lupus" was active in her body again, so her husband took her back to the hospital and he gave her a Bible study book. He said to Candiz, "in this book there is a chapter about healing, please read it." She told him to put it on the night table that she will read it later."

As the evening came, Candiz remembered that before her accident she had gone to see an evangelist from Puerto Rico. That night he shared his testimony that he had suffered from an incurable disease for many years. At the end of the service he began to pray for the sick, at that moment Candiz said to herself how can this man pray for the sick if he is sick himself? Here she was in a hospital bed with an incurable disease, asking herself how can she pray or lay hands on anyone that needs healing. She was devastated and cried all night long. The next day as she meditated on the Lord in the quietness of the hospital room, she heard from the Lord, and He said to her, "As you pray for the sick you will receive you're healing." Then she turned and saw the book which her husband had brought to her she read the book, deep down she was angry, hurt and always in pain. She studied the word so much, but here she was in "limbo." It does not matter how much you think you know about God's Word when you are diagnosed with an incurable disease it devastates your whole state of mind.

Many of her family and friends were not able to understand why this would be happening to Candiz when all she did was help so many people. Her father was so involved in their ministries, but he became angry at God when she got sick. He lifted up his fist saying. "How can you do this to someone that has served you so much?" Candiz told her dad not to be angry at God because He knew better. "God is faithful, merciful, and He will never leave me nor forsake me!"

Candiz had spent thirty-three years away from her father and never wanted to be far away from him again; nevertheless at that time of her life she was very successful. She made a big decision to buy him a home in Long Island close to her house; which was just a town away. He got involved in their ministry and finally became a big part of their lives. Candiz finally got to know what kind of man her father was, and the best part is that had finally stopped drinking. For three years he helped her at home and the homeless ministry they went to several places in NYC feeding the Homeless. He was a kind and loving man, always telling Candiz stories about his relationship with her mother. He expressed the fact that he still loved her. The pain in his heart was still fresh and painful because of the separation. Nothing was able to mend his broken heart, the love for her mom was strong. They both learned that if God loves us… we must love one another.

Not with hypocrisy, but with a caring love that only comes from God.

CHAPTER SIX

Abide In The Lord

If ye abide in me, and my words abide in you, ye shall ask what ye will, and it shall be done unto you. (John 15:7, KJV).

As Candiz began to study the book her husband had previously brought to her, something happened to her. It was like God used her husband to wake her spiritual understanding from a slumber of depression. There in the hospital room Candiz, began to realize that she was a Christian that knew and studied the word of God, but she wasn't using it to help herself. She let herself die spiritually for a time, no matter how many times she went to church, or how many times several pastors prayed for her to receive healing. They all advised Candiz to fight for her life, but it didn't make a difference to her until the day when she read the book about abiding in God. She was in the hospital room gazing at her book and those words resounding in her memory over and over again. *"If you abide in me and my words abide in you; then and only then asked whatever you want and it will be done unto you."* Wow, it was there all the time, and she had missed it.

What is it with people who are spiritual leaders, knowing the word of God, that when they go through horrible illnesses they act like they have been defeated?

The next day a doctor examined Candiz, and he noticed that she had some problems with her heart. He ordered the nurse to transfer her to the heart monitoring floor for observation. She'd wondered what was wrong again with her. As the hours pass bye, her emotions got the best of her, she became so angry and tired of being in the hospital. She began to pray and thank God, it was nothing serious. The next day as she continued to read the study book she felt so much better, that her doctor send her home. Candiz was on so many medications that she was not able to think straight. Being sick so much got to her so badly that she found herself being angry all the time. She became hard to live with; nevertheless everything around her was collapsing, and she didn't care. The only good thing was that no matter how she felt, when Candiz got home from the hospital, faithfully she would always go to church. The love of God was always within her heart, deep down in her heart she knew God loved her, and He was never going to let her go. One day Candiz and her children went to church, and when they returned to their house her husband was gone. She was hurt and very angry at first. As the days went by, the anger turned into hate; because when she needed him the most he had left them.

She began to use higher doses of pain medication so she wouldn't be able to think about anything. Candiz was trying to numb all the feelings of hurt from within her, and all the circumstances surrounding her life. But God would not let her destroy her life. Jesus Christ was always there for her every step of the way.

Candiz's husband was gone, and she was not able to work or afford the mortgage any longer. A short time later she and her children got evicted from their home. However a miracle happened! God provided a house for them "glory to God"! After several months, Candiz's husband called her and asked her for forgiveness. He stated that he wanted to come back, but she responded very angrily; "forget about me and start looking for somebody else; because I never want to see you again." Many months went by, and all she wanted was for the pain to stop. She didn't know what to do? That feeling felt like it was killing her inside because she was active in church, and she knew that she was not able to function right with this kind of feelings in her heart. A couple she was helping made her believe that her husband was no good, that he was holding her back from really functioning the way God wanted her to function. As Candiz thought back about everything, she ask herself, "What in the world happened to me?" It was like she was a piece of bread in the hands of God being broken piece by piece; or she felt like a blob of clay on the potter's wheel being formed into His likeness. Although she felt like her whole life was coming to an end; nevertheless God was creating a woman after His own heart. Every tear every circumstance in her life, every pain God would use it for His glory later on in her life.

After ten months, she ended up in the hospital with so many complications. One of them was internal bleeding. This time the doctors informed Candiz that they had to do an operation to stop the bleeding. She had so many medical problems that she didn't think she was going to make it; so she decided to call her sister and asked her to, please take all her children home to her house. Candiz even gave her a letter giving her custody of them. Twenty-six day after the surgery she found herself still in the hospital. The father of her primary physicians came to visit her in the hospital, and he said these words, "Our dear Lord cannot let all this happen to you now. "He said to Candiz", you have children and they need you"! For some reason those words kept replaying in her head, "her children needed her". What was she doing giving up? Candiz stated these words over and over "I have to live for my children." Something happened within her spirit; because all she wanted to do was to focus only on God. She began to pray and as she cried to the Lord, asking Him to "forgive her" for always doing things her way, she made a promise to the Lord, that she would no longer lean on her own understanding but in all her ways she will acknowledge Him Lord of her life. (Proverbs 3:5-6)

Candiz was praying asking God to please direct her path. After the surgery, it was hard for her to sleep. She turned on the television and saw a Pastor preaching about seeking God first before we do anything, she immediately got off the hospital bed and fell onto her knees. Candiz began to cry and began talking to God, saying to Him to please give her another opportunity to do everything he wanted her to do. She exclaimed that her life was no longer hers, but His. The first thing God told her was to forgive and to go get her husband. That was <u>not</u> something she wanted to do! The second thing God told her was to move to Orlando Florida, another thing she did not want to do. In order for her to have a new beginning she had to obey God. For almost a year, she maintained hatred and anger in her heart toward her husband for abandoning them, and that's when they needed him the most.

But slowly God removed all those horrible feelings from her heart and filled her with so much love and concern for her husband. For three years, her eldest son practically begged Candiz to move to Orlando. Nothing anybody would say would make her move. But when God commanded her to go to Orlando Florida, it puzzled her a little at first because to her, it was a little strange? You see Candiz's husband lived in another part of FL and God was sending her to Orlando. Although it hurt to leave New York, Candiz still had to obey God in everything He wanted her to do. A week later she was discharged from the hospital with a new way of thinking.

Never again will she ever be leaning on her own understanding, but in all of her ways she had to acknowledge God as her Lord. She felt God leading her every step. Candiz left the hospital, rented a van, packed it with a few things and headed to pick up her children from her sister's house. Her sister convinced her to stay with her for a little while, and she did. But Candiz had the mandate from God to go to Orlando. All of a sudden; it was like all hell broke loose for four days straight. Candiz's sister and her husband were at war; everything was going wrong she felt like Jonah in the boat. It felt like every person in that house was in a horrible storm, and the only way to calm the storm was for Candiz to go. Candiz quickly told her children to get everything ready; because it was time to go: An eighteen-hour ride turn into a five-day nightmare.

Little did Candiz know, that God was working patience into her children's and her lives throughout the five days? Three times as she was driving Candiz fell asleep, nearly having a head on collision with two different vehicles, but thank God nothing serious happened to them. The children were fighting in the car and made it so difficult to for Candiz to continue driving. Many times they had to stop so they could rest. But on the fourth night of their adventure the children were playing and arguing with each other; therefore Candiz began to pray. She rebuked every evil spirit that was trying to stop them from getting to Orlando. Candiz told the kids to get out of the van for a little while. Looking at her children as they all played on the grass, God placed an idea in her head. Suddenly she asked her children to get back in the van. Candiz said, "Now kids I want you all to sing praises and worship songs or the rest of the way to Florida. They did; and they finally got there!

God was preparing every single one of them for a new life in Orlando FL, and they didn't have any idea of what to expect when they arrived. Candiz didn't have a clue of what, why, or where God was sending her, because Orlando is a big place. What does this have to do with love? Nothing, but then again it has everything to do with it. You see, we must understand that there is always somebody that truly loves us. Sometimes we go through depression or loneliness. During that time, it is easy to come to the conclusion that nobody in this world loves us. However, I'm here to tell you that this is not true. There is always someone that loves you. You see, God created mankind with that void in their hearts on purpose.

God never intended for a man or woman to be away from Him. He knew that man was going to one day drift away from Him. The only way men would return to Him was by feeling loveless, and lonely. Nobody would be able to take God's place in another's heart. The void within is what God uses to get His creation back! God loved His creation so much that He would never give us up; because true love never gives up on you no matter how many mistakes you commit.

In the Bible it says, "We all have sinned, and we come short of the glory of God." (Romans 3:23). "God sent His only Son Jesus Christ that whosoever believe in Him will not perish but will inherit eternal life." (John 3:16). We must follow two commandments in order to live a life full of love. The first one is Matthews 22:37-39. "Jesus said unto Him, Thou shalt love the Lord thy God with all thy heart, and with all thy soul, and with all thy mind." Jesus himself gave us all this great commandment. My question to you is, "Do you love God that way? When we begin to love Him this way, the love of God will overtake us, something inside of us will start happening. We'll begin to feel love we'd have never experienced before, the true love that only come from the Father up above.

I promise you that when you begin to love God with all of your heart, mind, soul, and might. Every relationship we'll have on earth will be a better one because finally the void within our hearts will be filled with the one that is the perfect fit in that empty part of our life. This brings me back to a song that goes like this... "I love Him, I love Him, because He first loved me, and He purchased my salvation on a Calvary's tree." Yes, He loved us first. In the book of Jeremiah, 31:3 we read, "The Lord, hath appeared of old unto me, saying, Yea, I have loved thee with an everlasting love. Therefore with loving-kindness have I drawn thee?" (KJV). The void in our heart is used to draw us back to Him. We must understand that without God's love… life feels empty, without meaning. We must learn to love God with all our hearts; which is the first commandment. Let me tell you an amazing secret when we truly love God with our whole heart no one could hurt, or destroy us. You know why? Because when our hearts is full of love for God, it will not matter what horrible things people do to us. For a moment, we all will feel some emotion, but rapidly we will feel sympathy about that person. Because they lack God's Love; that helps us to love one another.

His love leads the way to better understand the mystery of the unsearchable riches of Christ (Ephesians 3:8). They are unsearchable because we are too busy looking for love in all the wrong places. When we finally come to that point of loving God with all of our heart, soul, mind and strength. We will understand, what Paul meant when he said these words. "And to make all men SEE what is the "fellowship" of the Mystery, which from the beginning of the world hath been (hid in God), who created all things by Jesus Christ. (Ephesians 3:9)

"By" used especially with passive verbs, for showing who does something or what causes something. What is this mystery that have been hidden in God from the beginning of time? Don't you want to know? The mystery is "LOVE" of Father God with His creation. Love that Saves. Love that Heals. Love that restores and maketh Alive. True and real Love that no storm, earthquake, natural or human disaster can touch.

Don't you want this kind of Love? Let me tell you that from the beginning of time, there was a fellowship between God and His creation (the human race) that was broken; when Adam and Eve disobeyed God. Ever since thousands and thousands of years ago. God's main purpose is to have that same fellowship with every single one of us again. Paul's prayer tells us in (Ephesian 3:13-14) that we be strong, and that we faint not. That we may live and practice the mystery that have been hiding all of these thousands of years. People been looking for satisfaction in people and things, but at the end still feeling so empty inside. The relationship between a husband and wife destroyed because some way, somehow they felt that "their" personal need to be loved in their special way was not met.

Parents are giving up on their children because they have gone wild, disrespectful, and out of control. Co- workers are always fighting for higher positions so that they could feel more important? (Ephesians 3:16- 20) We read that "He (God) would grant you, according to the riches of His glory, to be strengthened with might by His Spirit in the inner man; That Christ may dwell in your hearts by faith, that ye, being rooted and grounded In LOVE. May be able to comprehend with all saints what is the breadth, and length, and depth, and height; And to know the LOVE of Christ, which passeth knowledge that ye might be filled with all the fullness of GOD. Now unto Him that is able to do exceedingly, abundantly above all that we ask or think, according to the power that worketh in us." (KJV) And the second commandment is like unto it,

"Thou shalt love thy neighbor as thyself." (Matthews 22:39 KJV)

You might say, who is my neighbor? The answer is everyone we come in contact with... the person within your house. The people living not only in your street, but also the ones that sit next to you on the bus, or train. Even the ones next to you in the pews at church, supermarket, doctor's office, place of work, etc. Now the question is? "Do we love ourselves"? Because if we don't we will never learn to love the way God intends for us to love one-another. God's love in our hearts is the real love, God is love; He is the creator of everything. His love is perfected in us day by day as we spend time with Him. In the Book of (Romans 8 verses 35-39) we read, "Who shall separate us from the love of Christ? Shall tribulation, or distress, or persecution, or famine, or nakedness, or peril, or sword? As it is written, for thy sake we are killed all the day long; we are accounted as sheep for the slaughter. Nay, in all these things we are more than conquerors through Him that loved us."

"For I am persuaded, that neither death, nor life, nor angel, nor principalities, nor powers, nor things present, nor things to come, nor height, nor depth, nor any other creature, shall be able to separate us from the love of God; which is in Christ Jesus our Lord". When we understand this kind of love, we will know how to love our neighbor. Now over twenty-seven years has gone by, and after so many circumstances and trial, tribulations nothing could separate Candiz from the true love that only comes from God. She can say and mean it with all of her heart. Jesus Christ is the true and real love we all been searching for all of our lives. Jesus Christ gave His life for you and me, He did not have to do that, but He did because he truly loves us. Believe me when I tell you, all you have to do is spend enough time in prayer and reading the Bible. An acronym I learned a few years back to be a great description of what the Bible is and should be to us all.

> Basic
> Instructions
> Before
> Leaving
> Earth

We will never feel lonely or loveless again because we have a promise that says; "let your conversation be without covetousness, and be content with such things as ye have: for He hath said, I will never leave thee, nor forsake thee. (Hebrews 13:5 KJV) By experience I know that He will never leave us, you might ask what happened to Candiz when she arrived in FL. Read on;

When Candiz arrived in Orlando FL, it was a miracle, after so many difficulties getting there. She ended up homeless with her children and grandchildren, but on that precise day a man approached her and said that he will pay for their hotel stayed. She was stunned but so grateful to God for providing a place to sleep for them. Candiz saw a big empty pool in front of her hotel room door; therefore every day early in the morning. She would rise at 4:30 Am to pray and seek for answers and direction from the Lord. As to where he wanted her to go. For many years, Candiz did most of her ministry work at the largest Sunday school in the world. To Candiz's surprise, one day when she went back into their hotel room her daughter stated that a man in a wheelchair came by to invite them to a church program the following day which was Saturday.

She woke up the next day to do the usual praying this time asking God to show her where it is that he wanted her to go. After praying Saturday morning, God answered her prayers. He sent a man in a wheelchair, inside a yellow bus inviting them to go to church with him. God led Candiz to the place he wanted her to be; little did she know that He was going to use what was familiar to her, to accomplish his purpose. After the program, the yellow bus took them back to the hotel. Another challenge threatened Candiz's path:

True Love at Last

Candiz lost their room because the hotel owner didn't want them to keep their little dog. So again they almost ended up in the streets, but God send an angel in a wheelchair to rescue them, he took them to another hotel and paid for a whole two weeks. Plus he gave them a vehicle to use. God used this man to help Candiz. May the Lord bless him forever and ever? Candiz's eldest son asked her to go live with him till she gets herself together, and they did. He took them to an amazing church in FL; which they all loved. But this was not the church God had led Candiz to, but He did lead her to the other church in soon after that… But it took her several months. By that time, Candiz and her children already had an apartment and were more stable. She felt the leading of the Holy Spirit directing her to become a member of the church. They all went forward and became members.

God used Candiz in many ways helping people learn how to have a personal relationship with Him. By living out the words of God by example. God has used her for His honor, and his glory bringing hundreds of people to a closer relationship with the Lord. In 2007, Candiz and her husband started a ministry that has been used by God to bring hundreds and hundreds of people to the Lord… are you ready? Yes in "Orlando FL".

In this church, Candiz met an amazing group of people who love her unconditionally. She has learned perseverance, obedience, and to love one another the Way God commands us all to love each other. In this Century-year-old church, God used Candiz to coordinate the first Women's Conference in the history of the church. Her passion has been to bring many to the saving knowledge of Jesus Christ.

God has truly blessed her with an opportunity to reach thousands of people every week through public media. As Christians, we need to understand the dos and don'ts of the love God offers us all. First of all… we must decrease and He increase in us. The best picture to describe the love we must have is in the following chapter. (Read on)

CHAPTER SEVEN

The Necessity of Love

Have you ever witnessed a person who professed to be a Christian? You hear them talking about how much they love God when they have never seen in person; then one day you see them mistreating another Christian? When our actions toward another person are not loving at all, it shows that the love of God is not in that person. (We must live, act, and breathe Love). Because God is love, those who claim to be born again must love everyone. He commands us to love one another. In the Bible, we read, in (John 13:35 KJV), "by this shall all men know that ye are my disciples if ye have loved one to another." Love the person, hate the sin. Love is the evidence which shows others that we are saved. My eldest son shared this poem with me when he was just a teenager, and I want to share it with you.

Love
It's a feeling that's real.
It's a feeling that's strong.
It's a feeling that you give to someone.
Only to someone that will always respect it,
Not to someone that will make you regret it.
Some people think that love is just a
word, a word that has no meaning.
But if only they knew how it could hurt,
bringing out emotions, and feeling.
Love is a word that could be stronger than life.
Some don't understand it, till a loved one has died.
If you have ever hurt because of love, I want
you to know there's a man (Jesus) up above.

A man that loves you with all of His heart, and will not let you down, nor give you a scar.

His name is Jesus, and He truly cares. He won't let you fall because He is always there.

The mind of a young man was expressing in his poem the love God has for us. My friend, it does not matter how much I know about God, or how much the Lord uses me in prophecy; it doesn't matter, how much understanding of His Word I know; even, if I have much faith, when I don't show love to my brethren, it's all vain. How can I say to God that I love Him so much when I have never seen Him but I mistreat the people around me whom I can see? This includes our families. This ought not to be. For God called us all to love one another and live in peace.

How can we exemplify this kind of love? Feeding the need and those less fortunate is one of my favorite things to do. Like me, on weekends Candiz and her husband went to what was called "Night Watch" to minister to homeless man and woman, offering them a warm Christian place to live with three meals daily. The meals were prepared by the greatest cook in the whole world Candiz's dad, who was in charge of the shelter's kitchen. He demonstrated God's love by feeding everyone on time, and he did it with so much joy, every single day as unto the Lord.

He also went along every time they had to help pack boxes of love for needy families or Easter candy for needy children from different churches. Those were the best years Candiz spent with her father. He moved to Long Island to help them with their church "New Beginning Ministries". Those were days that she will never forget. Every time she called him he responded by saying with excitement "let's go serve, the Lord." He had a wonderful loving heart, and he shared the love of God by helping and feeding those who that were in need. When her wonderful father went to be with the Lord, Candiz knew that Jesus had prepared a place for him in heaven.

As Christians, the love of God is within us. When we come in contact with those who are seeking for true love, it is easier to share the true love of God with them. True love changes things, people, and circumstances. So again, as a team they gave all to the poor with much love never expecting anything in returned. It's so important to do everything as unto the Lord with much love. "Hope maketh not ashamed; because the love of God is shed abroad in our hearts by the Holy Ghost, which is given unto us." (Roman 5:5 KJV). This love that is shed in our hearts by the Holy Ghost, comes from God. It is the true love for which everyone is seeking. However, seekers can only find it when they seek God. Loving someone this way means to have patience in your relationship, to be kind even if others are unkind. Never envy anything or anyone; instead encourage seekers to continue to do good, don't ever think highly of themselves, but be humble, and God will exalt them in due time.

Love Anyway
Even if you are not, love anyway,
Even when they hurt you, love anyway,
Even when they are rude, love anyway,
Even if they are unkind, love anyway,

> Even if we don't deserve what Jesus Christ
> did on the cross for you and me, He did
> it because He loves us anyway.
> (By Rosa Marti)

Try telling someone who has committed wrong against you these words: "I love you, and Jesus does too." By you living this kind of love, the person who is causing the wrong will stop, think about their actions, and hopefully change. Love is never selfish, loving someone just to see what you get for yourselves is not love. Giving of yourself and expecting nothing is called selfless love. When we truly love someone, even if they make a mistake, it does not diminish our love for them. The love will remain; but we will show a different attitude of grace. For some reason every time we get hurt we are provoked to think evil of the perpetrator; but just imagine if God would feel the same way about us? "Ouch!" We must never forget about His Mercy and grace; therefore we must show some mercy to those that cause us hurt.

"Love is patient." "Hmm"… what does this mean? Can it be that we will always deal with people who are not perfect? Oh, my, does it mean that we ourselves, are hard to get along with? Can we have a problem that others can see, but we are blind to our own actions? When we finally realize that we are not perfect, then we will be less judgmental of other's imperfections. Don't stop loving others when they seem different from you, or when they react to situations in a different way from you. Respect the uniqueness of those whom God created in His image. Respect that we are all made by an awesome God who is very longsuffering with our imperfections too. It will be a good idea to try our best to look at people through the eyes of God. If you have a problem understanding the meaning of seeing someone the way He sees us all, just know that is very hard to give up on somebody you truly love.

When you truly love someone, you will never wish them harm, nor will you ever talk evil about them. Don't ever laugh at another person's misery; you shouldn't get happy about somebody else's pain. That is not a sign of love. We are called to "rejoice with those who rejoice and weep with those who weep; rejoice with them that do rejoice, and weep with them that weep. (Romans 12:15, KJV).

> (1Corinthians 13:7, KJV) "Beareth all things, believeth all things, hopeth all things, endureth all things."

This scripture reminds me of my personal walk with Jesus. Through every circumstance, trial and every mistake I have committed, God loved me so much, He never left me alone. With His love, I learned to bear, sustain myself in Him, always depending and believing in his word. Hoping for a closer relationship on a daily basis, I realized that with Him, I can endure all things. A hard place to be is when someone we love and believes in, cause us harm. A Mother, a Father, a child, a friend, or a spouse, it's hard to withstand it. Nevertheless when we have the love of God in our hearts, we learn to forgive and forget more often. The more time we spend with God, the more we learn to love people. The more we pray for them, one day we will see God transforming their lives. With God all things are possible, so don't give up.

True love comes only from God. His love never fails, never gives up; it is a constant, a love which never ends. Everything ends; but true love lasts forever. God's love is eternal. Only Jesus, the Son of God, is perfect, in all His ways. It took for one who is perfect in love, to give and show us how much God truly loves us all. He didn't care how much He suffered; the love within Him was greater than the pain He endured for us. God's love was shed into our hearts (Romans 5:5)

1 Corinthians 13:8-10 (AMP)

Candiz says, "Oh, I will never forget the precious day when I first accepted the Lord Jesus Christ into my heart. I heard the preacher state that God loved me so much and that He gave His only begotten Son to die on the cross for me Wow what a sacrifice! I felt like the only one in the room; tears began to roll down my cheeks… God was calling me to Himself, and I responded to His call, and there in front of thousands of people I gave my life to Jesus… on that precise day I stop smoking cigarettes, and never started again. I realize that when we are first born, we are not born with a cigarette in our mouth. It was hard for the first 23 days, but Praise the Lord! I never smoked another cigarette again. My life, as a new believer began, reading and studying the Bible, which was and is a priority. It was a burning desire to know everything I could about God." As the days and years passed Candiz learned to put away childish behavior.

1 Corinthians 13:11 (AMP)

Candiz became a Bible teacher and she trains people how to grow in the word, and how to put those childish ways, that keep us away from fulfilling the call of God on our lives. The more time we spend studying the Word, the easier it gets to share His love with everyone. In the Bible we read, But be doers of the Word, [obey the message], and not merely listeners to it, betraying yourselves [into deception by reasoning contrary to the Truth]. (James 1:22-25 AMP)

For if anyone only listens to the Word without obeying it, being a doer of it. He is like a man who looks carefully at his [own] natural face in a mirror; for he thoughtfully observes himself, and then goes off and promptly forgets what he was like. But he who looks carefully into the faultless law, the [law] of liberty. And is faithful to it and perseveres in looking into it. Being not a heedless listener who forgets but an active doer [who obeys], he shall be blessed in his doing (his life of obedience).

For now we are looking in a mirror that gives only a dim (blurred) reflection [of reality as in a riddle or enigma]. But then [when perfection comes] we shall see in reality and face to face! Now I know in part (imperfectly), but then I shall know and understand fully and clearly. Even in the same manner as I have been fully and clearly known and understood [by God]. (1Corinthians 13:12 (AMP)

We don't know what the future holds for us all unless, we are born again and know that one day we will be face to face, with the one that gave his life for us. Can you imagine or try to picture the face of our Lord Jesus Christ? I just can't wait until that blessed day, when we all see His face; Ooh what a glorious day it will be, to finally see the man that set us free.

To live confidently, trust with expectations of fulfillment, without faith it is impossible to please God. We must have hope for to learn to wait for what God has promised; if we don't have love, we will live empty lives. We heard of Him, who is to come, the one that would cleanse us all, of our sins. We live waiting by faith, expecting to see Him one day. Our Heavenly Father up above taught us the greatest thing we all need, which is love. A love without measure, love that has no ending, love that burns within our hearts for everyone we meet. "Thank you, Lord" for revealing the true and real love that I have been searching, for so long. 1 Corinthians 13:13 (AMP)

CHAPTER EIGHT

True Love at Last

"Jesus answered her, all who drink of
this water will be thirsty again.
But whoever takes a drink of the water that I will
give him shall never, no never, be thirsty anymore.
But the water that I will give him shall become
a spring of water welling up (flowing, bubbling)
[continually] within him unto (into, for) eternal life.
The woman said to Him, Sir, give me this
water so that I may never get thirsty nor
have to come [continually all the way] here
to draw." John 4:1-43 (AMP) read it.

What an amazing story about the Samaritan woman at the well of Jacob. Many of us have heard different interpretations of this story from the pulpit. The subject of a woman with divers' man in her life is questionable for many. There are also many judgmental ironies spoke about this unique woman that had five husbands, and the fact that the one currently living with her was not her husband. It was so interesting when Jesus talked about water that He offers and in-turn ask her to go get her husband, and He will tell her about this water? Was this the ultimate test of integrity? Jesus knew everything about her, and she had the opportunity to hide her secret past.

But when Jesus confronted her with her past He didn't judge her for the many men that were in her life, she responded with the truth. Something is so special with this encounter, between a sinner and her savior. Jesus saw a woman that was looking for love in all the wrong places. This story doesn't tell us the details of her past, but we do know the details that lead her to her destiny.

This story talks about a woman with five failed marriages; the story does not inform us if this woman had any children? We don't know if this woman was ever abused as a child. Was she a woman that was hurting at the time of this encounter? Jesus saw her heart; He was not interested in her past sins, but she was because of the excitement she showed when Jesus revealed to her about those five husbands. He knew that His Father in heaven used broken vessels. That day at the well of Jacob, she met her true love, the one she was searching for her whole life. Something within her began to flow, which is called the living water of the gospel of her Lord and Savior Jesus Christ. Now she knew the truth that set her free. She had to let it out, or she was going to explode. Therefore, she ran so fast that she forgot her water bucket; she was no longer thirsty; because she had an encounter with the living waters, and she knew that her soul will never thirst again. She was so much in Love with Jesus that she became the first evangelist in Bible history and brought many unto the Lord. She finally felt loved by someone that was never going to leave her, nor forsake her, nor abuse her in any way shape or form.

True love my friend, is that we laid down our life for a friend. True love is when you meet Jesus, and make Him Lord of your life. And you make the decision to walk in Love with him every single day. This love is the kind that overwhelms your whole insides; it makes you just burst like old wine skin, every time you meet someone it compels you to share the gospel or explode. True love is sharing the truth that will set them free, telling them that is not a religion but a true relationship with the King of Kings and Lord of Lords Jesus Christ. True love is caring for a soul so much that you must do everything possible to rescue them from the fires of hell.

Dear friends, we just go through so many situations in this world that we try to build relationships with people, rather than building a relationship with our maker. God is love, and those that dwell in Him live in His love; you might be asking, how can we live in God? I'll tell you by living a life completely surrendered to God, offering Him the first minutes of our everyday life. I'm not saying to forget about everybody or everything around you, I'm just saying, give God time "first" before you do anything else. Pray- Prayers gets you closer to a Father-son/daughter relationship. Worship draws you to His presence. When we face problems in our lives, our emotions run wild. When this happens, it's good to turn on Praise and worship songs and began to sing unto the Lord.

So many trials and tribulations most of us had to endure but is always good to remember a special scripture in Psalms 34:19 (KJV). Many are the afflictions of the righteous: but the LORD delivered him out of them all. And God has done just that for a multitude of people!

After a year of Candiz and her husband reconciled and they decided to renew their marriage vows and serve their Lord and Savior Jesus Christ together as one. They are both directors of Sidewalk Sunday School Ministry going to the highways and byways preaching the gospel in the streets of Orlando Fl. Together they now know that the more they love God with all of their hearts, soul, mind and might (strength) they will be able to love each other, and those closest to them. It has truly been a new beginning for Candiz's marriage. Everything is so much better now. They are using the word of God in their relationship when the struggles come; they claim Gods word in their situation. They also pray for each other, and most every night since they met each of them pray together for their children, families and friends. I truly believe that the more we let go of the self (what about me syndrome) and concentrate on God, the better life will be.

I thirst for Jesus, and when I seek Him with all of my heart, this thirst get satisfied with everything that is within me and being satisfied with him alone. You see, in the Bible the book of John chapter 4 Jesus talked to the women at the well, He asked her for water and she questioned him, why was he speaking to a Samaritan woman? This question was strange to her because the Jews would not speak to the Samaritans. This story touched me in such an amazing way especially when he told her these words "when you drink the water from the well you will thirst again, but when you drink the water I give… You would never thirst again".

I know many people will want to find this water? You just got to picture yourself with a very thirsty throat in the middle of a desert. The Sun is beaming down on you, and all you want is the water from a well, pond, or even from the clouds to quench your thirst. But I want to talk to you today about a thirst for more of Jesus. Look at your life right now is it empty, dry? Are you seeking fulfillment in things that really at the end of the day does not last, or matter? The water that Jesus gives runs inside your belly like rushing rivers that are like adrenaline in your being. After you drink this water, your life will never be the same. Nothing will be more important to you than fulfilling the call that flows from your spirit.

Do yourselves a favor; accept Jesus today as your Lord and Savior, and let Him fill that void in your heart with what has been missing all this time, "His Love". When I first came to know Jesus, I went to visit a little Spanish Church. They were singing a song that goes like this. "To love only you Lord, and never look back, I will keep following your steps, Lord. I will keep following you, and I will not faint, bowing before your altar Lord, and I will never look back."

This song became my prayer. I would only love Him, and no matter what happens I was to continue my journey with Him, till the end and never turn back. Open your heart to Jesus, and I promise, Jesus will take care of you; nevertheless just when you think that everything is over, God will let something fresh begin deep within you… that void in your heart will be gone.

If you have never made Jesus, Lord of your life? This day is a great opportunity for you to do that. Say these words; Father God, I come before you Lord, asking you to forgive me all of my sins, cleanse me from all unrighteousness, and make me brand new. Father, I believe that you send your son Jesus to die on the cross for me because you loved me so much, thank you, Father, for loving me unconditionally in Jesus Name Amen!

Now that you have received Jesus into your hearts you need to find a Church fellowship that preaches the powerful word of God. I call it the ones that preach about Jesus and teach you to become a doer of the word and not a hearer only. When you get ready spiritually and biblically, God will use you to share His word and the true love that only comes from Him. Jesus commands us to go and teach all people to observe all things whatsoever I have commanded you: and, lo, I am with you always, even unto the end of the world Amen. (Matt 28:20)

Now, my prayer is that you have received the Lord as your Lord and Savior. As Christians, we must study the Word of God to show ourselves approved unto God a workman, needed not to be ashamed rightly dividing the word of truth. (2Timothy 2:15, KJV). The more we study the Bible, the more we will learn to share the gospel with others. Everyone is called to share the good news of Jesus Christ, by using our individual talents given to us by God!

You'll be surprised that the very thing you do best in your spare time could indeed be use to bring someone to Jesus Christ. People all around the world use colors to described the plan of salvation. Others put quilt blankets together to give to sick people in the hospitals. In different ways, we can show that there is someone out there that cares. Showing true love to others will most often free them from pain and bondage. Have you ever wonder why a baby cries when they get hurt and immediately when we kiss their booboo they stop crying? (I call it the power of love and caring.)There are many individuals that feel lonely with a great void in their hearts; sometimes living a life that so many people around them ignored their existence. This situation makes them not care about themselves or anyone else.

Beloved, let us love one another for love is of God and everyone that love is born of God, and knoweth God. (1John 4:7) The main purpose of this book is to lead you to the only true love that you have been looking for all of your life. God is that love, and you could only have access to God through Jesus Christ.

"Jesus saith unto him" I am the way, the truth, and the life: No man cometh unto the Father, but by me John 14:6 (KJV). In the Bible we read; The word is near you, even in thy mouth, and in thy heart: that is, the word of faith, which we preach; that if thou shall confess with thy mouth the Lord Jesus, and shalt believe, in thine heart that God hath raised Him from the dead, thou shall be saved. For with the heart man believeth unto righteousness; and with the mouth confession is made unto salvation. (Romans 10:8-10 KJV).

I give to you all these scriptures that will help you grow and see how it all fit together to lead you to reach others for the glory of God;

Beloved, let us love one another: for love is of God; and every one that loveth is born of God, and knoweth God. He that loveth not knoweth not God; for God is love.

In this, the love of God was manifested toward us, because that God sent his only begotten Son into the world, that we might live through him.

Herein is love, not that we loved God, but that he loved us and sent his Son to be the propitiation for our sins.

Beloved, if God so loved us, we ought also to love one another.

No man hath seen God at any time. If we love one another, God dwelleth in us, and his love is perfected in us. At this moment know we that we dwell in him, and he in us, because he hath given us of his Spirit. And we have seen and do testify that the Father sent the Son to be the Savior of the world. Whosoever shall confess that Jesus is the Son of God, God dwelleth in him, and he in God.

And we have known and believed the love that God hath to us. God is love; and he that dwelleth in love dwelleth in God, and God in him.

Herein is our love made perfect, that we may have boldness in the Day of Judgment: because as he is, so are we in this world.

There is no fear in love, but perfect love casteth out fear: because fear hath torment. He that feareth is not made perfect in love.

We love him because he first loved us.

If a man say, I love God, and hateth his brother, he is a liar. For he that loveth not his brother whom he hath seen, how can he love God whom he hath not seen?

And this commandment has we from him, that he who loveth God love his brother also. 1 John 4:7-21 (KJV)

True love comes from the creator of heaven and earth. This same Creator created you, me, trees, flowers, animals, fish, sun and salvation through His Son Jesus Christ!

He said that He knows us before we were in our mother's womb. Thus saith the LORD, thy redeemer, and he that formed thee from the womb, I am the LORD that maketh all things; that stretcheth forth the heavens alone; that spreadeth abroad the earth by myself; Isaiah 44:24 (KJV)

Before I formed thee in the belly I knew thee, and before thou camest forth out of the womb I sanctified thee, and I ordained thee a prophet unto the nations.

Then said I, Ah, Lord GOD! Behold, I cannot speak: for I am a child.

But the LORD said unto me, Say not, I am a child: for thou shalt go to all that I shall send thee, and whatsoever I command thee thou shalt speak.

Be not afraid of their faces: for I am with thee to deliver thee, saith the LORD.

Then the LORD put forth his hand and touched my mouth. And the LORD said unto me, Behold, I have put my words in thy mouth. Jeremiah 1:5-9 (KJV) And God has done just that, and I have put it on paper for all of you that want that void filled.

In conclusion, Love is the key to peace in all of our circumstances. Let us love one another and help people to rise to a higher level with the right relationship, first with Abba Father and then with others. Love is infectious and the greatest healing energy. My question to you today is, how you want to be love unconditionally or with a condition? There is nothing you have to do for God to love you. When you get filled with the love that God gives nothing else will matter. You will never expect this kind of love from anyone else because God's Love complete us all. Love conquers all things. The word of God states that love covers a multitude of sins (1Peter 4:8). He is not just referring to all our sins; nevertheless He is also referring to the sins of the whole world; He is talking about those sins that others commit against us. Let me tell you about three important truth that will help you live better lives.

1) We must Love God with all of our Hearts (Mark 12:30-31)
2) We must Love our neighbor (Matthew 22:39)
3) We must Love one another (John 13:35)

Loving God with all of our hearts does not prevent us from loving others, on the contrary, it helps us to love them well. Walking in love with God will help us grow in the kind of person God wants us to be. Loving God with all of our hearts, protects our hearts and emotions from being destroyed. You might ask how we obtain that kind of love. I call this;

"Love breaks our legs" (Just picture Jesus with the lamb around His neck)

Jesus loves us so much, that He never wants for us to miss the life that God has intended us to live. Many times we don't understand the loneliness we feel, or why people we love turn their backs on us, especially when we need them the most? Or why accidents, disease, illness decides to give us a personal visit? In that very moment, we are forced to stay put, for an indefinite period. The pain in our mortal body will not let us move. I call this time in our life (Jesus broke our legs so we could listen and spend intimate time with Him. There in the quiet surrounding of our hospital or home bedroom we are consumed with sometimes unbearable pain, or maybe mistakes that we have committed ourselves that has taken our freedom… we call upon Jesus.

Love has broken our legs and opened wide our ears to hear in silence His small still voice. In that place of loneliness, pain, and confusion; God reaches down, because now He has our full attention. Instead of questioning or blaming God for what has happened to us? Let us surrender, submit and ask Him "Lord what are you trying to tell me. Please speak Lord" the longer we remain in His presence, the aroma of His love will enter our nostril into the inner yearning of our souls. Finally there in that circumstance we will understand that He and He alone is God and we are not. There at that moment, is when everything that surrounds us become a shadow in the light of Him. We forget the loneliness and the pain in the aroma of His love. We will understand that nothing else matters, but being in His presence all the days of our lives. "Truly my soul finds rest in God," (Psalm 62:1). With all of my heart, I pray that this book and the story of Candiz will transform your life with the true love, OUR LORD AND SAVIOR JESUS CHRIST!

About the Author

Rosa Ortiz Marti is the Founder of "Women of Prayer Removing Mountains and New Beginning Ministries. She is the mother of seven amazing Children and eight grandchildren; she has participated in ministry work for the past 27 years. Her ministry work began at Metro Christian Center where she found salvation. Metro Christian Center (The world largest Sunday school) is a non-profit organization dedicated to serving inner-city children in NYC and abroad. Their mission is to find and rescue inner-city children in the urban environment. Together with her Husband Pedro Marti they reach thousands of children and adults through various reach-out ministries. They Co-Direct the Sidewalk Ministry of FBCWP FL. Rosa loves the word of God and uses it to help transform lives by sharing it with everyone she comes in contact with every single day. She loves teaching children and women and has had the honor of helping many women who once depended on the government for financial help to become self-sufficient. She reached out and helps those who are hurting and abused, with the goal that every single one of them become mentally healthy again.

She is currently pursuing her Doctorate Degree in Biblical Studies and Religion at Liberty University.

CPSIA information can be obtained at www.ICGtesting.com
Printed in the USA
BVOW03s0131200516

448879BV00001B/20/P